S

by Dr. Harold J. Berry

Former Professor of Bible & Greek
Grace University
Omaha, Nebraska

BACK TO THE BIBLE
Publishing

MORMONS
published by Back to the Bible

International Standard Book Number
0-8474-0821-3

For information:
BACK TO THE BIBLE
POST OFFICE BOX 82808
LINCOLN, NEBRASKA 68501

Printed in the USA

MORMONS

"I asked the Personages who stood above me in the light, which of all the sects was right—and which I should join. I was answered that I must join none of them, for they were all wrong."[1]

So begins the account of the history of one of the largest religious groups in the world today—the Church of Jesus Christ of Latter-day Saints, more commonly known as "LDS" or "Mormons." According to Joseph Smith, the founder and "prophet," when he was only 14 years old he received this vision while praying for wisdom in the woods of upstate New York in 1820. Having been "called" by God to form His "only true church," Smith reportedly was directed by an angel to a set of golden plates containing God's true revelation, which he translated with the help of two magical stones. This translation—known as the *Book of Mormon*—along with many subsequent "revelations" given to Smith, became the basis for many of the beliefs still taught by the Mormons today. Even current president Gordon Hinckley said, "doctrines won't change," as he was installed as the LDS president on March 18, 1995.[2] Yet, as we will see later, Mormon doctrines (teachings) have changed over the years, even though they are supposedly received as revelation from God, who does not change (Heb. 6:17-18).

Mormonism is one of the fastest-growing religions in the world. In 1986 world membership was at 6 million.[3] In a decade, membership has increased 50 percent, to 9 million! That includes 4.8 million members in 10,218 groups in the United States.[4]

Much of this tremendous growth can be attributed to the church's aggressive missionary outreach. Mormon teenagers are expected to dedicate two years of missionary service on a self-supporting basis. Currently the group has more than 40,000 missionaries (up 10,000 since 1986) working throughout the world.[5]

This growth, coupled with its requirement that each member tithe 10 percent of his income, has made the church one of the wealthiest organizations in the United States. Reporting for *Time*, S. C. Gwynne and Richard Ostling point out that in 1996 the LDS had an estimated annual income of $5.9 billion, of which $5.3 billion was from tithes and offerings, and assets worth $30 billion.[6] Gwynne and Ostling conclude: "If it were a corporation, its estimated $5.9 billion in annual gross income would place it midway through the Fortune 500.[7]

In addition, the Mormons wield a great deal of social and political influence. A number of key business and political leaders are Mormons, as well as several popular entertainers and athletes. In contrast to the Jehovah's Witnesses, who refuse to salute the flag or serve in the military, there are many Mormons among military personnel.

Background

To understand Mormonism, we must first look at the life of the founder, Joseph Smith Jr., for he is at the center of Mormon theology. The Mormons believe that Smith was God's prophet. Their faith is based on the revelations he supposedly received from the Lord. Yet there is even debate about what the Mormons call the First Vision that he received, referred to at the beginning of this booklet. Former Mormon Janis Hutchinson points out there are three versions of the First Vision: "1832 account—Jesus only; 1835-36 diary—Angels only; 1838 account—God the Father and Jesus."[8] Hutchinson concludes, "Smith just couldn't keep his stories straight. To make matters worse, Mormon leaders insist that 'during

Joseph Smith's lifetime, he told but one story.'"[9]

The importance Mormons place on Joseph Smith is clearly seen in statements they have made about him. For instance, Brigham Young, the second president of the church, wrote of Smith: "Whosoever confesseth that Joseph Smith was sent of God . . . that spirit is of God; and every spirit that does not confess that God has sent Joseph Smith, and revealed the everlasting Gospel to and through him, is of Antichrist."[10] Such a statement is highly significant when we realize that a president of the church is considered the prophet who speaks for God. The Mormon home page on the Internet has the heading "Continuing Revelation," under which is written, "Divine revelation for the direction of the entire Church comes from God to the President of the Church. The Presidents of the Church down through the years since it was restored in 1830 have been and are viewed by Latter-day

Saints as prophets in the same sense as are Abraham, Moses, Peter, and other such biblical leaders."[11]

Through the years the Mormons have maintained that Smith possessed a flawless character. Brigham Young boasted, "Examine the character of the Savior, and . . . of those who have written the Old and New Testament; and then compare them with the character of Joseph Smith, the founder of this work . . . and you will find that his character stands as fair as that of any man's mentioned in the Bible. We can find no person who presents a better character to the world when the facts are known than Joseph Smith, Jun., the prophet, and his brother Hyrum Smith, who was murdered with him."[12] When the facts are known about Joseph Smith, however, we see that his character and life were far from perfect.

Joseph Smith was born into poverty in Sharon, Vermont, on December 23, 1805. When Joseph was 10, the family moved to Palmyra, New York. Smith's father "was a mystic, a man who spent most of his time digging for imaginary buried treasure (he was particularly addicted to Captain Kidd's legendary hoard)."[13] At that time, treasure hunting was a common pastime. Frequently, money diggers would use "peep stones" or "seer stones" to search for buried treasure. According to former Mormons Jerald and Sandra Tanner, "These stones were sometimes placed in a hat and used to locate buried treasure."[14]

Joseph often joined his father and brother Hyrum in searching for buried treasure. In fact, it appears that his interest in money digging was even greater than that of his father. The evidence also indicates that he made frequent use of seer stones and other occult articles in searching for treasures for himself and for others. The Tanners cite a number of examples of Smith's money-digging activities. Their book also includes a photograph of a court document that "proves that Joseph Smith was a 'glass looker' and that he was arrested, tried and found guilty by a justice of the peace in Bainbridge, New York, in 1826."[15] Fawn M. Brodie also reproduced this and other records in her revealing biography of Joseph Smith.[16]

According to Mormon records, Joseph Smith's revelations and visions began at an early age. When he was 14, Smith reportedly became concerned about which denomination he should join. (He had been impressed with Methodism, but later his family converted to Presbyterianism.) After reading James 1:5, which instructs any who lack wisdom to ask God for it, the future prophet went to the woods to pray. As he prayed, he was supposedly overcome by an enemy spirit. Suddenly two "personages" appeared, causing the enemy spirit to flee. One of the personages addressed Smith and—pointing to the other personage—said, *"This is My Beloved Son. Hear Him!"*[17] (emphasis his). The personages then proceeded to tell Smith that all of the churches were wrong and that he should not join any of them. Thus, Mormons would have us believe that, with one vision given to a 14-year-old boy, God wiped out 18 centuries of historical Christianity.

Three years later, at the age of 17, Smith supposedly received the extraordinary revelation that became the basis for Mormonism. As he lay in bed praying, the angel Moroni reportedly appeared to him and told him where to find some buried golden plates that contained the history of ancient America. The heavenly messenger added that on the plates was written "the fulness of the everlasting Gospel, … as delivered by the Savior to the ancient inhabitants."[18]

Since these plates were supposedly written in "reformed-Egyptian characters" (a nonexistent language), the angel told Smith that he would also find a pair of transparent stones set in silver bows (like spectacles) to use in translating the plates. When Smith found the plates, however, he was not allowed to take them but was told to wait four more years. Finally, in 1827, after the angel had made several more appearances, Smith was allowed to take the plates with strict instructions to keep them hidden.

In 1829 a teacher named Oliver Cowdery visited Smith and was soon converted to the new religion. Cowdery then became Smith's scribe. As Smith gazed through the stones (known as the Urim and Thummim), the reformed-Egyptian hieroglyphics would appear to him in English. He would then read the translation to Cowdery, who would record it. Cowdery and the other helpers never saw the plates, however, for the helpers were always separated from Smith by a screen or curtain.

About a month after Smith and Cowdery started the translation, they were supposedly visited by John the Baptist, who told them to baptize and lay hands on each other, thus ordaining themselves into the Aaronic priesthood. Later, Peter, James and John appeared and ordained them to the Melchizedekian priesthood.

In 1830 the translation (called the *Book of Mormon*) was published. On April 6 of that year, 24-year-old Joseph Smith and five other men officially organized what would later be named the Church of Jesus Christ of Latter-day Saints.

Shortly after this first official meeting, Smith and his followers moved west and settled in Kirtland, Ohio. In Kirtland the first quorum of 12 apostles was chosen, with Smith as the president. In June 1831, God supposedly commanded the followers of Smith to settle in Missouri, the "land of Zion." (The LDS presently own 14,465 acres in Jackson County, Missouri, where Jesus will supposedly return to set up His kingdom.[19]) A number of Mormons moved to Missouri, while the rest remained in Ohio. Smith went from one locality to another because he was accused of many misdeeds, including immorality.[20] It seems that Brigham

Young and others had a higher view of the character of the first president than did some Mormons of Smith's day.

During the next few years, the followers in both locations, now numbering several thousand, were at odds with the non-Mormons. In Missouri, after several clashes, the Mormons were finally forced to flee the state in 1838. They also had been driven out of Ohio. Smith eventually led the majority of the group to Commerce, Illinois, which he renamed Nauvoo. Smith was Nauvoo's mayor. It was here that Joseph Smith joined the Masonic Lodge, explaining many similarities between Mormon and Masonic rituals.[21] The Tanners conclude, "Although Mormon apologists would have us believe that Joseph Smith received the temple ceremony by revelation from God, the evidence is against it and clearly shows that he borrowed heavily from Masonry."[22]

Persecution from non-Mormons and unrest within the church continued to hound Smith, largely due to the "revelation" that the prophet received in 1831 establishing the practice of polygamy. Sources differ on how many wives and children Smith had, but a conservative estimate is 20 wives and 47 children.

In 1844 Smith entered national politics by becoming a candidate for president of the United States. A newspaper started by some excommunicated Mormons, *The Nauvoo Expositor*, exposed the Mormons' polygamous practices and criticized Smith's political aspirations. In essence, the paper put Smith on trial in the eyes of his followers. A group of Smith's followers broke into the newspaper office, destroyed the press and burned copies of the paper. Joseph and Hyrum were arrested and placed in a jail in Carthage, Illinois, to await trial. However, three days later (June 27, 1844), a mob stormed the jail and killed both Joseph and Hyrum.

After the death of Joseph Smith, a struggle ensued among his followers regarding who would succeed him.

Brigham Young, president of the Twelve Apostles, managed to keep the majority under his leadership, but several splinter groups developed. Even today there are various groups among the Latter-day Saints. According to the *Handbook of Denominations in the United States*, there are Latter-day Saints (Mormon), Church of Christ (Temple Lot), Church of Jesus Christ (Bickertonites), Church of Jesus Christ of Latter-day Saints (Strangite), and the Reorganized Church of Latter-day Saints.[23]

Brigham Young eventually led the largest group of the Latter-day Saints westward to the valley of the Great Salt Lake in what would later be known as Utah, arriving in 1847. In 1997, the Mormons commemorated the 150th anniversary of those who trudged the Mormon Trail with a wagon train reenactment of the trek from Omaha to Salt Lake City. But 150 years ago the Mormons were not receiving the positive press that they are today. In those days they were actually trying to get outside of the United States. Utah was not a state then and it wasn't allowed to become one until the Mormons officially renounced their practice of polygamy. In 1890, 59 years after the first president/prophet received the revelation authorizing polygamy, another president/prophet—Wilford Woodruff—rescinded it. Six years later, Utah became a state.

The second-largest group of Joseph Smith's followers settled in Independence, Missouri, and called themselves the Reorganized Church of Jesus Christ of Latter-day Saints (RLDS). In contrast to the 4.8 million followers of LDS in the United States, there are only about 150,000 of the RLDS.[24] The church in Missouri chose a son of Joseph Smith for their leader. They were referred to as "Josephites," because they believed a descendant of Joseph Smith should be the head of the church. Those who followed Brigham Young were referred to as "Brighamites."

The RLDS does not want to be confused with the LDS; that is, the Missouri followers of Joseph Smith are adamant about not wanting to be identified with his Utah followers. They do not use the name "Mormon" and differ with the Mormons on several issues. In addition to disagreeing over prophetic succession, the Reorganized Church rejects the historical practice of polygamy. Specifically, they do not believe that Joseph Smith practiced it, which is difficult to maintain in the light of evidence presented by the Utah Mormons and by a number of other historical documents and books. Both groups follow the *Book of Mormon* and the other writings of Smith in addition to the Bible. Both believe in continuing revelation. Both also regard the teachings of "Prophet" Joseph Smith to be divinely inspired and to be the foundation of their beliefs.

Much more could be written about both groups and about the specific beliefs of the Missouri followers, but this discussion of beliefs will be limited to the Latter-day Saints (Mormons).

BELIEFS

The beliefs and practices of the Mormon church bear little resemblance to the teachings in God's Word or to the practices of the early church. On its Internet home page, it says, "The Church is Christian but is neither Catholic nor Protestant. Rather, it is a restoration of the Church of Jesus Christ as originally established by the Savior."[25]

Mormons added the phrase "Latter-day Saints" to their name to indicate their belief that they are a latter-day restoration of the church that Jesus Christ personally established while He was on earth. They teach that, after Christ ascended, He visited the American continent and preached the Gospel to the ancient inhabitants. He then instituted the doctrines and practices of His "true church," which were duly recorded on the golden plates.

However, the people were destroyed before they could establish the new order, so the world had to wait 1,400 years for this restoration to take place.

Mormons believe their mission is "proclaiming a new dispensation, the restoration of the priesthood and rituals of the 'true church,' and the eligibility for the attainment of deity by all Mormons."[26]

Source of Authority

In addition to the Bible, the Mormons have three other volumes that they believe contain revelations from God—the *Book of Mormon, Doctrine and Covenants* and the *Pearl of Great Price.* The Mormon scriptures are held in higher esteem than the Bible, for Mormons follow these three books even if the teachings in them contradict the Bible. And there are many contradictions.[27]

The Mormon church says, "*The Book of Mormon: Another Testament of Jesus Christ* is divinely inspired scripture, as is the Holy Bible."[28]

The Bible is placed in a weakened position among Mormon scriptures by their eighth Article of Faith, which states, "We believe the Bible to be the word of God as far as it is translated correctly; we also believe the Book of Mormon to be the word of God." To say the Bible is the word of God "as it is translated correctly" allows Mormon leaders to reject the Bible whenever they wish.

The main story in the *Book of Mormon* covers a period of 1,000 years, from 600 B.C. to A.D. 400. The Introduction to the *Book of Mormon* says, "The book was written by many ancient prophets by the spirit of prophecy and revelation. Their words, written on gold plates, were quoted and abridged by a prophet-historian named Mormon. The record gives an account of two great civilizations. One came from Jerusalem in 600 B.C., and afterward separated into two nations, known as the Nephites and the

Lamanites. The other came much earlier when the Lord confounded the tongues at the Tower of Babel. This group is known as the Jaredites. After thousands of years, all were destroyed except the Lamanites, and they are the principal ancestors of the American Indians."[29]

This introduction to the *Book of Mormon* also quotes Joseph Smith's words: "I told the brethren that the Book of Mormon was the most correct of any book on earth, and the keystone of our religion, and a man would get nearer to God by abiding by its precepts, than by any other book."[30] But notice what the publishers are forced to admit in the comments about this same edition of the *Book of Mormon*: "Some minor errors in the text have been perpetuated in past editions of the Book of Mormon."[31]

Think about it. Even the Mormons admit that errors have been perpetuated in the *Book of Mormon*! And how interesting that the publisher calls them "minor errors." With the claims the Mormons make for the writings of Joseph Smith, there are no such things as minor errors. An error is an error. Yet the Mormons don't even cite an example of these "minor errors."

The historical accuracy of the *Book of Mormon* presents an interesting problem. The Mormons claim the *Book of Mormon* is a history of ancient America, but non-Mormon archaeologists find no support for such a claim. Letters from qualified sources make such statements as "The book [*Book of Mormon*] is untrue Biblically, historically and scientifically," and "The Smithsonian Institution has never used the Book of Mormon in any way as a scientific guide. Smithsonian archeologists see no direct connection between the archeology of the New World and the subject matter of the book."[32]

The *Book of Mormon* has not been found accurate in its historical comments either as a guide to exploration or in agreeing with known history. If a book is to guide us in truths about the world we have not yet seen, then surely it should be accurate when it speaks about the world we have seen. By contrast, the Bible has been used as such a guide in archaeological exploration in the Middle East, particularly in Palestine. The Bible has been found to be geographically and historically accurate. It is expected, of course, that those who refuse to accept the Bible as final authority would also seek to discredit archaeological discoveries that confirm its truths.

Another difference between the Bible and the *Book of Mormon* is the original language. The inspired text of the Bible was given by God to the authors in the common language of the people, whereas the *Book of Mormon* was supposedly translated from Egyptian hieroglyphics. It seems strange, therefore, that many passages in the *Book of Mormon* are exactly as stated in the King James Version of the Bible published in 1611. Walter Martin has documented some of these passages.[33] According to Martin, the *Book of Mormon* contains at least 25,000 words from the King James Bible.

Many people believe that the actual basis of the *Book of Mormon* was a book written by Solomon Spaulding (also spelled "Spalding") entitled *Manuscript Found*—rather than a supernatural revelation as the Mormons claim. This is the belief of the three authors of *Who Really Wrote the Book of Mormon?* Their evidence includes testimonies, handwriting analyses and statements from Smith and Spaulding and their relatives.[34]

Another important debate is over the "Book of Abraham," which is a part of the *Pearl of Great Price*, accepted by the Mormons as scripture. The "Book of Abraham," supposedly written by Abraham himself, gave the Mormon church its anti-black doctrine. (The church taught until 1978 that black people were under a curse and could not serve in the priesthood.) It has now been established—although understandably not accepted by the LDS—that the "Book of Abraham" was not written by Abraham himself. Even the Reorganized Church of Latter-day Saints (RLDS) seems to accept this, but not the Utah Mormons.[35]

The Tanners, former Mormons themselves, say, "We feel that if any person will honestly examine this matter he will see that the evidence to disprove the 'Book of Abraham' is conclusive. We have shown that the original papyrus fragment Joseph Smith used as the basis for the 'Book of Abraham' has been identified and that this fragment is in reality a part of the Egyptian 'Book of Breathings.' It is a pagan text and contains absolutely nothing concerning Abraham or his religion."[36]

For a church whose presidents/prophets still receive revelation from God, who does not change, it is interesting that a "new" revelation was received in 1978 reversing the previous revelation about blacks being cursed and not worthy of priesthood privileges. Although the church has been evasive about how the new revelation was received, it did reverse the previous revelation.[37]

The Mormons place all of their scriptures (including not only the *Book of Mormon* but also *Doctrine and Covenants* and the *Pearl of Great Price*) above the Bible in authority. Wallace Bennett has said, "We recognize the Bible's limitations as well as its value. We do not ascribe final authority to any of its statements because we believe that God has reestablished the authority to speak in His name, and has given it again to righteous men. Obviously, we do not accept the idea that with the adoption of the present contents of the Bible the whole canon of scriptures was closed for all time."[38]

Writing from the viewpoint of the Latter-day Saints, Steven Shields says, "One of the most important doctrines for both the RLDS church and LDS church is that the canon of scripture is not full—that God continues to direct the church through revelation to the prophet."[39]

By placing their presidents/prophets as the source of authority in directing the church, the Mormons thus reject the Bible as final authority and as such are not in line with biblical Christianity.

GOD

The Mormons hold many doctrines that are contrary to the Word of God. Their beliefs about the Person of God are at great variance with what God has revealed about Himself in the Bible. The Bible teaches that God is one, yet He exists in three Persons—Father, Son and Holy Spirit. According to Walter Martin, "Mormon theology . . . is polytheistic, teaching in effect that the universe is inhabited by different gods who procreate spirit children which are in turn clothed with bodies on different planets, 'Elohim' being the god of this planet (Brigham's teaching that Adam is our heavenly Father is now officially denied by Mormon authorities, but they hold firm to the belief that our God is a resurrected, glorified man)."[40]

Regarding the Father, the Bible says that He is spirit; therefore, He does not have a physical body. Jesus told the Samaritan woman, "God is Spirit, and those who worship Him must worship in spirit and truth" (John 4:24). The Mormon scriptures say, however, "The Father has a body of flesh and bones as tangible as man's."[41] Joseph Smith believed that God "was once as we are now, and is an exalted man."[42] He taught that God had once dwelt on a planet as a man and that through self-effort He eventually became God. This led Smith to teach that all good Mormons could become gods: "You have got to learn how to be Gods yourselves; to be kings and priests to God, the same as all Gods have done."[43]

When current president/prophet Gordon Hinckley was asked by *Time* reporters Gwynne and Ostling about the Mormon doctrine of man becoming gods, Hinckley "seemed to qualify the idea that men could become gods, suggesting that 'it's of course an ideal. It's a hope for a wishful thing,' but later affirmed that 'yes, of course they can.'"[44] How could the president/prophet, who is supposed to speak with the certain voice of God, be so uncertain?

Nor did Hinckley appear definitive when asked about the Mormon teaching that God was once a man. "I don't know that we teach it," he responded. "I don't know that we emphasize it . . . I understand the philosophical background behind it, but I don't know a lot about it, and I don't think others know a lot about it."[45] This side-stepping answer doesn't sound like one who is supposed to speak for God in articulating the doctrines of the church.

Mormon theology humanizes God and deifies man. Orson Hyde, a contemporary of Joseph Smith who was also a theologian recognized by the

Mormon church, said, "Remember that God, our heavenly Father, was perhaps once a child, and mortal like we ourselves, and rose step by step in the scale of progress, in the school of advancement; has moved forward and overcome, until He has arrived at the point where He now is."[46]

Such views reveal that the Mormon scriptures not only add to the Bible, but they also often contradict what the Bible clearly teaches.

CHRIST

Regarding the deity of Christ, the Mormons are far from being in agreement with what the Scriptures teach. Mormons teach that all men existed in eternity as spirit beings before they were given physical bodies. They believe Christ was simply a spirit being like the rest of us before He came to the earth. On the one hand, the Mormons ascribe deity to Christ; on the other hand, they bring Him down to a human level. Mankind is placed on the same level as Christ. According to *Doctrine and Covenants*, Jesus said, "I was in the beginning with the Father, and am the Firstborn. . . . Ye were also in the beginning with the Father."[47] The Mormons believe Christ was created in the same sense that we were created; in fact, they believe Lucifer (the Devil) was a "son of God" even as Jesus was a "son of God."

The Bible, however, teaches that mankind did not exist in eternity past. Man did not exist until he was created by God (Gen. 1:26-27). By contrast, Christ was not created; He did exist in eternity (John 1:1, 14).

Mormons are also unscriptural in their view of the virgin birth of Christ. Brigham Young stated, "He [Christ] was not begotten by the Holy Ghost.... Jesus, our elder brother, was begotten in the flesh by the same character that was in the garden of Eden, and who is our Father in Heaven."[48] Walter Martin therefore concludes that the Mormons believe the "Savior was produced, not by a direct act of the Holy Spirit but by actual sexual relations between 'an immortal or resurrected and glorified Father,' and Mary. . . . There can be no mistaking the fact that the Adam-god doctrine is meant here, no matter how vehemently the Mormon apologists of today may deny that it was ever taught."[49]

David Reed and former Mormon John Farkas comment about the Mormons' Adam-God: "Joseph Smith's successor, Brigham Young, taught that Adam (Eve's husband) is God—the only God worshiped by the Mormons. The LDS Church leadership today publicly repudiates this doctrine, and most Mormons are unaware that Brigham Young actually taught it throughout his presidency."[50]

The Mormons do not believe in the virgin birth of Christ. Ed Decker, a Latter-day Saint for 20 years who is now seeking to reach Mormons with the Gospel, says of the god of the Mormons: "He is said to physically live with His many wives near the star Kolob, where he procreates spirit children with his wives through natural means. Mormonism teaches that this god came down to earth in the flesh and was the physical father of Jesus."[51] This teaching opposes the scriptural teaching that Jesus was conceived by a direct act of the Holy Spirit (Matt. 1:18, 20; Luke 1:35).

The Mormons, in keeping with their doctrine of "plural marriage," or polygamy, believe that Jesus Christ was a polygamist. In the Mormon scriptures, it is "revealed" that unmarried people, and couples whose marriages are not sealed by the temple endowments, can become only "angels in heaven."[52] If their marriages are sealed, "Then shall they be gods."[53]

If, therefore, Christ had not married in this life, He would not have been able to rise above the position of an angel in the next life. Brigham Young believed that Jesus Christ was a polygamist. He believed that Mary and

Martha (the sisters of Lazarus) and Mary Magdalene were the wives of Christ. Young also taught that the bridal feast in Cana of Galilee was the occasion of one of Christ's own marriages. And remember, Prophets Smith and Young were "prophets in the same sense as are Abraham, Moses, Peter, and other such biblical leaders."[54]

Once again the teachings of the Mormons stand in sharp contrast to what is taught in the Bible. Nowhere does the Bible teach polygamy. Although some men in Bible times had many wives, this was not God's will, according to Deuteronomy 17:14-18. Instead of polygamy, the Bible teaches the sacredness of the commitment of one man and one woman to each other until death separates them (1 Cor. 7; 1 Tim. 3:2; Titus 1:5-6). It is interesting that some Mormons now deny that their church ever taught this doctrine.

Also, nowhere in the Bible do we find any evidence to support the idea that Christ was married—let alone that

He had more than one wife. It is obvious that the Mormons have rewritten the Bible to match their theology rather than taking their theology from the Bible.

SALVATION

The crucial doctrines of any religious group are what they teach about the Person of Christ and about salvation. What they teach in these two areas reveals whether or not they are following the Bible. Concerning salvation, the Bible says, "For by grace you have been saved through faith, and that not of yourselves; it is the gift of God, not of works, lest anyone should boast" (Eph. 2:8-9). John 1:12 tells us that we become the children of God by receiving Christ as Savior by faith. Obedience and good works are evidence that a person has trusted Christ for salvation, but they are not a means of salvation. Because salvation is a gift, it cannot be earned.

Mormonism, however, teaches that in addition to necessary faith, salvation is earned by works. The LDS third article of faith states, "We believe that through the Atonement of Christ, all mankind may be saved, by obedience to the laws and ordinances of the Gospel."[55]

For the Mormons, salvation depends on their works. This is evident from their doctrine of baptismal regeneration—the teaching that a person cannot be saved without being baptized with water. They say, "As stated by Joseph Smith, the first principles and ordinances of the gospel of Jesus Christ are, 'first, Faith in the Lord Jesus Christ; second, Repentance; third, Baptism by immersion for the remission of sins; fourth, Laying on of hands for the gift of the Holy Ghost' (Articles of Faith 1:4)."[56]

The Mormons even teach that salvation will be available in the next world to those who have not become

Mormons in this life. Because they teach that water baptism is necessary for salvation, however, they also teach that those who are alive should be baptized for the dead so that those who have believed after death can become Mormons. This means that a Mormon would be baptized for his own salvation and again for someone deceased.

A verse the Mormon church uses concerning its belief in baptism for the dead is 1 Corinthians 15:29: "Otherwise, what will they do who are baptized for the dead, if the dead do not rise at all? Why then are they baptized for the dead?" There are several possible interpretations of what this verse means. The most likely one that fits the context—and harmonizes with the rest of the Bible—is that new believers were being baptized and were taking the place of older believers who had died. All of this would be meaningless if there were no resurrection of the dead.

To insist, however, that this baptism has merit for those who have died would contradict the clear teaching of the rest of the Bible. A person should not build a doctrine on one verse—and certainly not on one that could just as easily have another interpretation.

The Bible does not support the Mormon doctrine of salvation after death. Hebrews 9:27 says, "It is appointed for men to die once, but after this the judgment." Our only opportunity to trust Christ as Savior is while we are alive. Neither does the Bible support the idea that we must be baptized in order to be saved. We are saved by means of the death of Christ; He paid the penalty for our sins. Nothing can be added to what Christ has accomplished for us.

Heaven and Hell

Regarding heaven, the Mormons teach that it is comprised of three levels and that individuals will be graded as to what category of heaven they will enter. Section 76 of *Doctrine and Covenants* teaches that there is the celestial kingdom, the highest level, which is prepared for the righteous who have been faithful in keeping the commandments of the Lord and who have been cleansed of all their sins. Only Mormons will enter this kingdom, which is subdivided into three levels. Only those Mormons whose marriage has been sealed by the temple endowments will reach the highest level, where they eventually achieve godhood.

Then there is the terrestrial kingdom. Those who go there have lived clean lives but were not willing to receive the Mormon gospel or were not valiant in the faith. Also in this kingdom are those who refused to receive the gospel on earth but who accepted the testimony of Jesus in the spirit world.

The third division is the telestial kingdom, into which will go all those who have been unclean in their earthly lives. These subjects are placed in the telestial kingdom after they have been punished for a time for their sins.

Regarding hell, Joseph Smith essentially adopted the teaching of the Universalists—that all mankind will eventually be saved. The official Mormon position now seems to be that hell is the place for those who cannot be redeemed, who are called "sons of perdition." This group, however, is "but a small portion of the human race."[57] Because only a "small portion" is excluded from salvation, Anthony Hoekema rightly observes, "One could . . . call Mormons virtual Universalists since, according to their teaching, the vast majority of the human race will attain to some kind of salvation."[58]

The Mormons do not teach biblical truths regarding heaven or hell. The Bible nowhere teaches that heaven contains various levels or that all mankind will be saved. Instead, the Bible teaches that our eternal destiny is determined in this life by whether we accept or reject Christ's death and resurrection on our behalf. Those who accept the Gospel message go to heaven, while those who reject it go to hell.

In their attempt to prove that heaven has three levels, Mormons cite 1 Corinthians 15:40: "There are also celestial bodies and terrestrial bodies; but the glory of the celestial is one, and the glory of the terrestrial is another." But the context of this verse makes it clear that the apostle Paul was comparing the resurrection body we will receive with the earthly body we have now. He was not talking about two (and certainly not three) levels of heaven.

CONCLUSION

The Mormons follow the teachings of Joseph Smith and Brigham Young rather than the Bible. When Joseph Smith became a polygamist, he received a new "revelation" to replace his former revelation that had condemned polygamy. He also became a Mason and integrated much of the Masonic ritual into his temple ceremony, which contradicted his former condemnation of secret societies. What started out to be a "latter-day restoration" of Christ's "true church" has become latter-day confusion.

The Mormons have added many of their own doctrines to what is taught in the Bible, claiming that God did not close the canon of Scripture when the Bible was completed. God has a severe warning, however, to those who would add anything to His Word: "If anyone adds to these things, God will add to him the plagues that are written in this book" (Rev. 22:18).

Mormons clearly are not followers of the Christ of the Bible. The revelations they claim God has given them contradict what the Bible teaches about God, Christ, salvation, heaven and hell. If Mormons were Christians in the New Testament sense of the word, they would accept what Jesus Christ says about Himself and what He says about mankind. They would accept the fact that all of us have sinned and come short of the glory of God and that the only way to obtain salvation is by personally receiving Jesus Christ as Savior (Rom. 3:23; Acts 16:31).

The Mormons say of themselves, "The Church is Christian but is neither Catholic nor Protestant." Because they reject the teachings of biblical Christianity, to be intellectually honest the Mormons ought also to say that their church is not Christian.

SUMMARY

Name of organization:
The Church of Jesus Christ of Latter-day Saints

Also known as: Mormons, LDS

Founder: Joseph Smith Jr. (1805-1844)

U.S. Headquarters: Salt Lake City, Utah

Membership (1996): U.S.: 4.8 million
Worldwide: 9 million

Internet Home Page Address:
http://www.lds.org

Twist or Truth?

SOURCE OF AUTHORITY

Mormonism:

Believes that the *Book of Mormon, Doctrine and Covenants* and the *Pearl of Great Price* contain God's revelations just as the Bible does. Believes in continuing revelation; does not believe the canon of Scripture was closed when the Bible was completed. Views the Mormon presidents as prophets in the same sense as were Abraham, Moses, Peter and other such biblical leaders.

Biblical Christianity:

Believes the Bible alone is final authority. Believes the canon of Scripture was closed when the 66 books of the Bible were completed. Believes no one today is like the Old Testament prophets who received direct revelation from God.

GOD

Mormonism:

Teaches that He was once a man who, through self-effort, became God. Teaches that good Mormons become gods.

Biblical Christianity:

Believes God has existed in eternity past,

although the second Person of the Trinity became incarnate to die for the sins of mankind. Teaches that man can never become God.

CHRIST

Mormonism:

Denies His deity by teaching that He was simply a spirit being before coming to earth. Denies the virgin birth by claiming Jesus was conceived when Adam-God had sexual relations with Mary. Claims that Jesus was a polygamist.

Biblical Christianity:

Believes that Jesus Christ is God, the second Person of the Trinity. Believes that Jesus was supernaturally conceived by Mary through the Holy Spirit. Maintains Jesus was never married.

SALVATION

Mormonism:

Teaches that salvation is earned by works in addition to faith. Believes that you cannot be saved unless you are baptized with water for the remission of sins. Practices baptizing for the dead so that those who have believed after death can become Mormons.

Biblical Christianity:

Teaches that salvation is granted only by grace through faith alone in the Lord Jesus Christ. Teaches baptism is a public witness of salvation, not a requirement to be saved. Does not believe there is another chance for salvation after death.

HEAVEN AND HELL

Mormonism:

Believes in three levels of heaven: Celestial, where good Mormons enter and achieve godhood; Terrestrial, where those enter who are good people who do not comply with teachings of Mormonism; and Telestial, where those enter who have lived unclean earthly lives. Claims that the vast majority of mankind will be saved—believing in virtually universal salvation.

Biblical Christianity:

Believes hell is the future place of punishment for those who reject salvation through Christ. Although there may be different degrees of punishment, all will be punished for rejecting Christ. Claims salvation only for those who trust in Christ; all who reject Him go to an eternal hell.

RECOMMENDED READING

Decker, Ed. *Decker's Complete Handbook on Mormonism.* Eugene, Ore.: Harvest House Publishers, 1995.

Enroth, Ronald, and others. *A Guide to Cults and New Religions.* Downers Grove, Ill.: InterVarsity Press, 1983.

Fraser, Gordon H. *Is Mormonism Christian?* Chicago: Moody Press, 1977.

Hutchinson, Janis. *The Mormon Missionaries: An Inside Look at Their Real Message and Methods.* Grand Rapids, Mich.: Kregel Resources, 1995.

Martin, Walter R. *The Kingdom of the Cults.* Minneapolis: Bethany House Publishers, 1985.

Mather, George A., and Nichols, Larry A. *Dictionary of Cults, Religions and the Occult.* Grand Rapids, Mich.: Zondervan Publishing House, 1993.

McDowell, Josh, and Stewart, Don. *Handbook of Today's Religions.* San Bernardino, Calif.: Here's Life Publishers, Inc., 1983.

Reed, David A., and Farkas, John R. *Mormons Answered Verse by Verse.* Grand Rapids, Mich.: Baker Book House, 1992.

Robertson, Irvine. *What the Cults Believe.* Chicago: Moody Press, 1991.

Scott, Latayne C. *Why We Left Mormonism: Eight People Tell Their Stories.* Grand Rapids, Mich.: Baker Book House, 1990.

Tanner, Jerald, and Tanner, Sandra. *The Changing World of Mormonism: A Behind-the-Scenes Look at Changes in Mormon Doctrine & Practice.* Chicago: Moody Press, 1980.

Van Gorden, Kurt. *Mormonism.* Grand Rapids, Mich.: Zondervan Publishing House, 1995.

White, James R. *Letters to a Mormon Elder: Eye-Opening Information for Mormons and Christians Who Talk with Them.* Minneapolis: Bethany House Publishers, 1993.

NOTES

[1] "Writings of Joseph Smith," 2:18-19 in *Pearl of Great Price* (Salt Lake City: The Church of Jesus Christ of Latter-day Saints, 1968), p. 48.

[2] *Christianity Today*, April 24, 1995, p. 45.

[3] Joseph Carey, "A Time of Turmoil for Mormons," *U.S. News & World Report*, April 28, 1986, p. 74.

[4] *The World Almanac and Book of Facts 1997* (Mahwah, N.J.: K-111 Reference Corporation, 1996), p. 644.

[5] Kurt Van Gorden, *Mormonism* (Grand Rapids, Mich.: Zondervan Publishing House, 1995), p. 16; as of Aug. 1, 1997, the LDS Internet home page claims "50,000 full-time missionaries serving throughout the world."

[6] S. C. Gwynne and Richard Ostling, *Time*, Aug. 4, 1997, p. 54.

[7] Ibid., p. 52.

[8] Janis Hutchinson, *The Mormon Missionaries: An Inside Look at Their Real Message and Methods* (Grand Rapids, Mich.: Kregel Resources, 1995), p. 100.

[9] Ibid.

[10] Brigham Young, *Journal of Discourses*,

Vol. 8, p. 176, cited by Jerald and Sandra Tanner, *The Changing World of Mormonism* (Chicago: Moody Press, 1980), p. 448.

[11] http://www.lds.org/Global_Media_Guide/Core_Beliefs_and_Doctrines.html, Aug. 1997.

[12] Brigham Young, *Journal of Discourses,* Vol. 14, p. 203, cited by Tanner and Tanner, *The Changing World of Mormonism*, p. 448.

[13] Walter R. Martin, *The Kingdom of the Cults*, 3rd rev. ed. (Minneapolis: Bethany House Publishers, 1985), p. 169.

[14] Tanner and Tanner, *The Changing World of Mormonism*, p. 78.

[15] Ibid., p. 67-68.

[16] Fawn M. Brodie, *No Man Knows My History: The Life of Joseph Smith* (New York: Alfred A. Knopf, 1985), pp. 20-21, 427-429.

[17] "Writings of Joseph Smith," 2:17, in *Pearl of Great Price*, p. 48.

[18] Ibid., 2:34, p. 51.

[19] Gwynne and Ostling, *Time*, Aug. 4, 1997, p. 55.

[20] See comments by Walter Martin, *Kingdom of the Cults*, p. 174.

[21] Tanner and Tanner, *The Changing World of Mormonism*, pp. 534-547.

[22] Ibid., p. 547.

[23] Mead, Frank S., rev. by Samuel S. Hill. *Handbook of Denominations in the United States, New Tenth Edition* (Nashville: Abingdon Press, 1995), pp. 165-172.

[24] *World Almanac and Book of Facts 1997*, p. 644.

[25] http://www.lds.org/Global_Media_Guide/Core_Beliefs_and_Doctrines.html, Aug. 1997.

[26] "Mormon," *The New Encyclopaedia Britannica, Micropaedia/ Ready Reference*, Vol. 8, 15th ed. (Chicago: Encyclopaedia Britannica, Inc., 1987), p. 328.

[27] For documentation see Einar Anderson, *The Inside Story of Mormonism* (Grand Rapids, Mich.: Kregel Publications, 1973), pp. 150-158.

[28] http://www.lds.org/Global_Media_Guide/Core_Beliefs_and_Doctrines.html, July 1997.

[29] "Introduction" in *The Book of Mormon* (Salt Lake City: 1981).

[30] Ibid.

[31] Ibid., "A Brief Explanation About

The Book of Mormon."

[32] Cited by Martin, *The Kingdom of the Cults*, p. 184.

[33] Ibid., p. 187.

[34] Wayne L. Cowdrey, Howard A. Davis and Donald R. Scales, *Who Really Wrote the Book of Mormon?* (Santa Ana, Calif: Vision House Publishers, 1980).

[35] Tanner and Tanner, "Fall of the Book of Abraham" in *The Changing World of Mormonism*, pp. 329-363.

[36] Ibid., p. 363.

[37] Tanner and Tanner, "Changing the Anti-Black Doctrine" in *The Changing World of Mormonism*, pp. 291-328.

[38] Bennett, *Why I Am a Mormon*, p. 159.

[39] Steven L. Shields, *Latter Day Saint Beliefs: A Comparison Between the RLDS Church and the LDS Church* (Independence, Mo.: Herald Publishing House, 1986), p. 22.

[40] Martin, *The Kingdom of the Cults*, p. 204.

[41] *Doctrine and Covenants*, 130:22.

[42] *Teachings of the Prophet Joseph Smith*, p. 345, cited by Martin, *The Kingdom of the Cults*, p. 202.

[43] *Times and Seasons*, Aug. 15, 1844, pp. 613-614, cited by Martin, *The Kingdom of the Cults*, p. 204.

[44] Gwynne and Ostling, *Time*, Aug. 4, 1997, p. 56.

[45] Ibid.

[46] Orson Hyde, *Journal of Discourses*, Vol. 1, p. 123, cited by Martin, *The Kingdom of the Cults*, p. 203.

[47] *Doctrine and Covenants*, 93:21, 23.

[48] Brigham Young, *Journal of Discourses*, Vol. 1, pp. 50-51, cited by Martin, *The Kingdom of the Cults*, p. 213.

[49] Martin, *The Kingdom of the Cults*, p. 213.

[50] David A. Reed and John R. Farkas, *Mormons Answered Verse by Verse* (Grand Rapids, Mich.: Baker Book House, 1992), p. 22.

[51] Ed Decker, *Decker's Complete Handbook on Mormonism*, p. 417.

[52] *Doctrine and Covenants*, 132:15-16.

[53] Ibid., 132:20.

[54] http://www.lds.org/Global_Media_Guide/Core_Beliefs_and_Doctrines.html, Aug. 1997.

[55] Article 3 of "The Articles of Faith of The Church of Jesus Christ of the Latter-

day Saints," *Pearl of Great Price*, p. 60.

[56] http://www.lds.org/Global_Media_Guide/Core_Beliefs_and_Doctrines.html, Aug. 1997.

[57] Hyrum Smith and Janne Sjodahl, *The Doctrine and Covenants Commentary*, p. 453, cited by Anthony Hoekema, *Four Major Cults* (Grand Rapids, Mich.: Wm. B. Eerdmans Publishing Company, 1963), p. 72.

[58] Anthony Hoekema, *Four Major Cults*, p. 74.